HOUSES NOW

living style

One's style is one's signature always.

Oscar Wilde

HOUSES

Edited by Sabita Naheswaran

NOW

living style

images
Publishing

Published in Australia in 2015 by
The Images Publishing Group Pty Ltd
ABN 89 059 734 431
6 Bastow Place, Mulgrave, Victoria 3170, Australia
Tel: +61 3 9561 5544 Fax: +61 3 9561 4860
books@imagespublishing.com
www.imagespublishing.com

Copyright © The Images Publishing Group Pty Ltd 2015
The Images Publishing Group Reference Number: 1156

National Library of Australia Cataloguing-in-Publication entry

Title:	Houses now: living style
ISBN:	9781864706161 (hardback)
Subjects:	Interior decoration.
	Architecture, domestic.
Dewey Number:	747

Coordinating Editor: Sabita Naheswaran

Designed by Ryan Marshall, The Graphic Image Studio Pty Ltd, Mulgrave, Australia
www.tgis.com.au

Pre-publishing services by United Graphic Pte Ltd, Singapore
Printed by Everbest Printing Co. Ltd., in Hong Kong/China
on 140gsm Chenming Snow Eagle Matt Art

IMAGES has included on its website a page for special notices in relation to this and
our other publications.
Please visit www.imagespublishing.com

Every effort has been made to trace the original source of copyright material contained in this book.
The publishers would be pleased to hear from copyright holders to rectify any errors or omissions.
The information and illustrations in this publication have been prepared and supplied by the contributors.
While all reasonable efforts have been made to ensure accuracy, the publishers do not, under any
circumstances, accept responsibility for errors, omissions and representations, express or implied.

CONTENTS

Axial Symphony	6	Design Systems Ltd
Curl Curl House	12	CplusC Architectural Workshop
Del Bosque	18	Pascal Arquitectos
Frangipani Residence	24	Paul Uhlmann Architects
CBI House	28	SGGB Architects
Garton St Residence	30	FORM architecture furniture
Goldsmith Residence	34	Abramson Teiger Architects
Bach House	40	Jamison Architects
Balmoral House	44	Fox Johnston
Casa Spodsbjerg	50	Arkitema Architects
House in Sai Kung	54	Millimeter Interior Design Limited
House No. 7	62	Denizen Works
Hunters Hill House	68	stanic harding architecture
House Val d'Entremont	74	Savioz Fabrizzi Architectes
Mirante do Horto House	80	FCstudio
Loft Apartment	86	Adrian Amore Architects
Madrona House	92	CCS Architecture
Mill Springs Ranch	98	Lake | Flato Architects
Moebius House	104	Tony Owen Partners
Altensteig House	110	Kauffmann Theilig & Partner
Claremont House	114	Brininstool + Lynch
Mothersill	120	Bates Masi Architects
Parede 11	126	Humberto Conde Arquitectos
Pearl Bay Residence	130	Gavin Maddock Design Studio
Pobble House	136	Guy Hollaway Architects
Santa Monica Canyon Residence	144	Griffin Enright Architects
Hog Pen Creek Residence	148	Lake | Flato Architects
Goodman Residence	156	Abramson Teiger Architects
Surf Residence	162	Paul Uhlmann Architects
Villa Le Trident	166	4a Architekten
Wollahra House I	174	stanic harding architecture
Ulm House	178	Kauffmann Theilig & Partner
Tennyson Point Residence	184	CplusC Architectural Workshop
St. Luke's	188	Morscher Architekten
Lakeshore Residence	192	Miró Rivera Architects
Planalto House	200	FCstudio
House in Shatin	206	Millimeter Interior Design Limited
R.J. Melman Residence	212	MOD Construction / Dirk Denison Architects
Mop House	216	AGi architects
McMahons Point House	220	stanic harding architecture
Wood House	224	Brininstool + Lynch
Hemeroscopium House	230	Ensamble Studio

A central axis, symmetry and spatial hierarchy have always been essential compositional elements in environmental design. Hong Kong studio **Design Systems Ltd** believes the creation of a symmetrical space can help people attain a state of mental equilibrium through its experiential and spiritual aspects.

Axial Symphony's functional spaces, furniture and fixtures are located on an axis projected from the most important spatial elements of that particular zone. This arrangement keeps the inhabitant physically and visually oriented to the centre of the various spaces and, consequently, always at the epicentre of a space. For example, the sink and the door of the bathroom are arranged on the same axis so that the basin is centred to the inhabitant once they enter the room. The garden is on the same axis with the window and sofas of the living room, meaning the landscape appears framed and centred in the window when inhabitants view that space from the sofas.

Design Systems Ltd used materials based on their compatibility to spatial function rather than their visual merit. White terrazzo was used for the flooring of the garden to highlight and expose the beauty of the undulating lawn and the vibrant surroundings while recycled boat-building timber was used in the living room to create a cosy and well-grounded interior.

9

13

Curl Curl House is a highly detailed and considered Australian building that responded to the client's brief, budget, seasonal climatic conditions and spatial goals. A shared driveway, a services easement and a compact site influenced the form of the building envelope, and allowed for the internal floor area to be maximised without sacrificing external amenity; at just under 100 square metres, every aspect of the design had to be carefully considered by **CplusC Architectural Workshop**. Plywood top and bottom plates were employed in conjunction with tightly spaced studs to achieve the dark cedar curve that leads to the main entrance.

With the existing shared driveway running past the living areas along the eastern facade of the dwelling, visual privacy became an important issue. Window openings along this facade were minimised, and cedar screens were integrated to prevent passers-by from peeking into living spaces. These screens – which were given a natural oil finish for added lustre – create modulation in the facade by breaking up the black cedar cladding with a warmer element; they can also be easily removed for maintenance.

To compensate for the minimal openings along this facade, a sinuous skylight runs the length of the eastern wall, allowing light to penetrate and permeate through living areas. The Laminated Veneer Lumber (LVL) beams forming the roof structure intersect the skylight on a rigorous grid, and required precise alignment with studwork to the external wall. Through careful detailing and craftsmanship **CplusC Architectural Workshop** transformed what would ordinarily be a concealed structural element into a striking design feature.

The client's specific requirement for the dwelling to be at one level informed the decision to raise *Curl Curl House* above street level, on par with the carport. Raising the floor structure meant a generous water storage system could be installed in the sub-floor space, and clean unobstructed spans in the living and private areas could be achieved. A construction system of continuous span LVL was used for both the floor and roof structure, with the roof beams being supported by a central spine unit that provides rigidity to the building and houses the service core of the home, incorporating wet areas, the living room joinery, wardrobe space and general storage. It also separates public spaces to the east from private spaces to the west.

Del Bosque, located in a wooded area with sloping ground and views to a golf course, is a contemporary Mexican-style residence, with a stone facade and terracotta-tiled roofs. All the materials utilised by **Pascal Arquitectos** are natural, and the environment resembles one of an old Mexican hacienda, with a cosy but contemporary garden that surrounds the entire property. The interior design fluctuates between Modern and Neoclassical styles, while the illumination is indirect, based on table lamps, standing lamps, buttresses and chandeliers.

The entrance presents a 'motor lobby' with a courtyard of squared arches made from quarried stone, and a cantilevered roof pierced by an oak tree, which leads to the common areas of the house. The entrance floors of red *pórfido* (porphyry) cobblestone complement interior walls finished with rustic stone, while the floors are of honed green slate.

Pascal Arquitectos used 20-inch-thick wooden beams within the structure to further emphasise the feeling of an old hacienda. The first floor was dedicated to common areas, comprising the kitchen and library, and living, dining, family and playing rooms. The upper floor includes more private areas, including the master bedroom – which is entered through a lobby and followed by a small living room – and three more bedrooms. The basement contains a movie theatre with deep leather and chenille sofas and a bar. Access to this room is via a wine cellar with a sophisticated seating space that includes six red leather chairs and a chandelier with red shades; this area also contains a kitchen and bathroom. Candles in wall recesses around the room add warmth and drama.

Designed by **Paul Uhlmann Architects**, this two-storey house takes complete advantage of its location in a beachside community located in northern New South Wales, Australia. Situated on the beachfront in a semi-tropical climate, the house pairs indoor and outdoor spaces to create a living experience perfect for the year-round mild climate the area offers. The contemporary resort feel of **Frangipani Residence** was realised through the use of a combination of materials and textures that evoke a sense of warmth and richness.

The main living areas, both internally and externally are located on the northeast corner to take advantage of solar access, and to allow for the penetration of cooling sea breezes in the hot summer afternoons. The exterior is a combination of free-form stone, rich timber cladding and rendered masonry. A similar mix of elements has been used internally, to create a warm backdrop to the strong external light. The palette, however, is more refined; a honed chocolate-quartzite floor is used throughout the ground level, and creates a subdued backdrop to the timber veneer cabinet panels. Externally, floor finishes are paved porphyry.

With its beachfront location, the design of the house caters for the use of the beach by the owners, with large areas for surfboard stores and wetsuit drying areas, as well as outdoor showers and spas. The interior embraces the view to the large tropical garden – as does a window seat in the lounge room – connecting to the lush green exterior via a series of framed windows. The main television is concealed above a fireplace adjacent to this area. A large two-storey void was incorporated into the design to link the private spaces on the first floor and the communal spaces on the ground floor. The building interiors were resolved with an in-house interior designer working hand-in-hand with the architect, while an external firm undertook the soft furnishing design once the building was complete. This led to a consistency in the detailing of the building that also complemented the intent of the original design.

Located in a dense forest near the Minte bridge in Puerto Varas, Chile, this 5,000-square-metre site presented **SGGB Architects** with the best type of soil to set up base in a topographically irregular sector with a low density of vegetation and a high level of natural light.

SGGB Architects sought to develop a house capable of optimising thermal criteria, and visually maximising the strata – both vertical and horizontal – of its surroundings. The design was developed based on a three-dimensional matrix of 1.5-metres-cubed – it was through this that spatial, structural, material and construction criteria were established. The resulting volume, **CBI House**, is defined mainly by the manipulation and combination of modules in three levels: public spaces at the first level (one unit), private areas on the second level (two units) and a bureau-hatch on the third level.

By means of a five-inch-squared wooden structure founded on concrete handcrafted benches, **CBI House** absorbs the topographical irregularities caused by the site's 15-percent slope. Morphologically **SGGB Architects** have sought to replicate strategies used in the 18th-century towers of Osorno, Chile, by constructing an entirely wooden structure with a compact programmatic distribution, and integrating sloped roofs to drain rainwater.

Despite its dark exterior of black-stained planks, large windows allow for plentiful daylight throughout and, on the north side, a canted wall was angled to allow room for skylights, which illuminate the lower floors. Above, prominent windows frame views of the forest setting.

29

In recognising that **Garton St Residence** (in Melbourne, Australia) was already well built, and that the client's requirements were modest and considered, **FORM architecture furniture** worked with the idea of reusing and replanning existing spaces and adding only an additional 8 square metres to the house, with a utility outhouse to the rear. The concept of sustainability merged with a shared interest in communal cooking, a fascination with craftsmanship, a taste for exotic patterns, an appreciation of sculpture and a love of wood. All of which were key to the design of this renovation.

The brief called for new kitchen, dining and sitting areas, a new bathroom, en suite, laundry and woodwork shed. The existing laundry / bathroom occupied a prime position at the back of the house. By giving that space back to the living room and moving the laundry outside the house, the additional living / kitchen space required by the family could be kept to a minimum. The 19th-century outhouses still visible in Melbourne's Carlton laneways came to mind when discussing where to locate the laundry. The possibility of combining it with a woodwork shed resulted in the design of a contemporary, multipurpose outhouse.

FORM architecture furniture saw no demarcation between interior and exterior, and designed the interior and exterior contemporaneously, facilitating a consistency between the two. Both utilise the natural beauty of timber as a dominant visual element. Timber was used to clad the new exterior walls, used extensively inside for cabinetry and ceiling lining and employed in a sculptural arrangement for a dynamic exterior awning – a wave form created by arranging identical sticks in a simple geometric pattern.

The kitchen cabinetry is dense with timber and displays a high degree of craftsmanship, finely detailed joints and an impressive slab top. This enthusiasm for timber is continued in the ceiling with its exposed timber joists, lining boards and herringbone struts. The ambience generated by the warmth and richness of timber results in a unique and deeply satisfying place to inhabit.

Set in the sweeping canyons of Beverly Hills, California, **Goldsmith Residence** is a modern interpretation of the traditional home. With its stunning vistas and wide sweeping spaces, this home is a centre of tranquility within the heart of the city. It embodies the qualities of the modern Southern California lifestyle fused with traditional elements.

Upon entry, one is met with grand windows with spectacular views of the surrounding landscape. The residence is approached via a winding driveway that curves across the property to conceal the main view of the residence. This graceful entryway encompasses trees and plants, harmonising the structure with the organic facets of the surrounding environment. The decomposed granite components provide the home with an estate-like feel, mimicking the detailed pathways of grand manors.

The two-storey living room features steel windows that allow for a slender profile extending across the edifice to unite the surrounding nature with the interior comfort of the home. Ample wall space creates a gallery-like setting perfect for presenting the owner's extensive art collection.

Abramson Teiger Architects sought to create a retreat from the hectic atmosphere of Los Angeles, promoting a resort feeling within the compound of the estate. Inside, areas such as the media room and master suite serve as centres of relaxation and serenity.

An emphasis on spatial expansion is evident in all facets of the design. All ground floor rooms have large openings that facilitate continuity within the floor plan. Outdoor living spaces take advantage of the Los Angeles cityscape. A cascading grass staircase leads to a pool nestled within the rolling hills of the property, while canopies set upon the landscape are ideal for entertaining. A detached garage integrated within the sloping topography of the locale compliments **Goldsmith Residence**. The structure contains a home office (on the lower level) with beautiful views conducive to a private and peaceful work environment.

Inspired by the Australian site and the client's lifestyle, personality and interests, **Bach House** was designed to embrace what was unique to its site, encompass passive environmental design principles and utilise materials that flowed seamlessly between internal and external spaces to diminish the presence of walls and strengthen the connection to the surrounding landscape. **Jamison Architects**' interiors and exteriors enhance and enrich one another, working simultaneously as one to create a unique, functional and aesthetically timeless design.

A magnificent 100-year-old fig tree in the centre of the site became the focal point for the design. From the view upon arrival at the entry to every living space in the home, views north towards the fig tree and surrounding hills beyond can be enjoyed. The northern aspect is maximised with an elongated plan containing a central spine that separates living areas to the north and wet areas to the south. Punctuated along the spine are courtyards and breezeways making the most of natural light and cross-ventilation. Along the central spine, sliding doors are used to contain or zone areas. Timber louvres used internally on bedroom walls also promote air movement when bedroom doors are closed.

The design of **Bach House** facilitates a strong connection to the landscape. Sitting lightly on the higher part of the site, the lawn mounds up gently from the fig tree to the central north-facing courtyard and deck. The difference between inside and outside is subtle and blurred due to the openness of the planning, extensive full-height glazing and the flow of materials used internally and externally. A creek bed that divides the site was embraced as another unique design aspect. Supported by V-posts, the wing end of the master bedroom cantilevers over the bank edge. When the creek is full, the trickle of flowing water can be heard from within the master bedroom further strengthening the connection to the site's landscape.

The architecture and interiors are unified with a refined palette of materials that were chosen for their textural qualities, colour and ability to be used both internally and externally. The four main elements used by **Jamison Architects** include timber decking and flooring, dark stained timber wall cladding, white plasterboard and painted plywood in the wrap-down roof form and coloured grey blockwork used for the garage, and as features to the internal fireplace and external barbecue. The western wall includes external decking that wraps up to form a balustrade; this continues inside to form the master bedroom bedhead and continues through to the en suite to become the vanity bench and joinery. Similarly the white form of the roof wraps down externally and internally to frame picturesque slot views to the west. Just as the flooring flows from the inside to the outside, the external wall cladding continues from outside to inside and runs the length of the hallway spine into the master bedroom.

Located above Balmoral Slopes in Sydney, the building takes the form of a series of platforms, responding to the rhythm and topography of the site. These platforms allow an interchange of levels throughout **Balmoral House**, creating privacy and interest between spaces. **Fox Johnston** orientated the building away from the street, with secluded living and sleeping spaces embracing the views and low-maintenance garden beyond.

Entry to the house is via an open courtyard leading to a transitional lobby space. This connects to upper and lower levels midway, designed specifically to facilitate a gentle change between the spaces in the building.

A long linear form to the west contains sleeping areas and bathrooms at the lower level, a garage space at an intermediate level and living areas and a media room on the upper level, where a linear courtyard provides a garden outlook, as well as a green view from the entry space. An elongated lap pool and spa bounds this form and bleeds into the entry space, forming a shallow pool at the entry courtyard. A cabana opens onto a large deck and pool, with a separate bedroom and bathroom above.

The upper-level roofs flip up to the north, with living spaces opening completely onto a northeast-facing deck; this volume was set in to allow an extruded skylight along the entry hallway below, which provides filtered light throughout the entire lower-level bedroom without compromising privacy. Sliding external walls and screens are an intrinsic part of the northern and eastern faces, allowing privacy and sun-control, as desired. The lower-level bedrooms lead onto private decks overlooking the garden, and the view beyond.

Balmoral House's narrow width and orientation allows for optimal cross ventilation and sun filtration. Bluestone walling forms the base of the building, as well as the basin of both the lap pool and spa. The upper volume of walling and screens is of Anthra Zinc panelling, interplayed with large sliding timber and glazed panels. These materials provide are environmentally responsive, allowing good thermal mass, keeping the building warm in winter and cool in summer.

Casa Spodsbjerg in Denmark was constructed on a plot facing the Storebælt that previously held a summerhouse from the 1920s. **Arkitema Architects** designed a residence that could house a growing family, and would function as an ideal setting for family weekends and holidays. The house's style can be described as New Nordic – a simple architectural design, which concurrently focuses on the human. The character and texture of the materials ensure personal and comfortable interiors – both concerning the architecture and the acoustics.

Design inspiration came from the previous building, which had grown organically to cover new needs and adapt to the site-specific qualities of the plot. **Casa Spodsbjerg** is made up of two parallel, staggered volumes that contain living rooms, bedrooms and bathrooms. The house sits on a tall base of in-situ cast concrete, containing a garage, basement, spa and a family room with sea views and access to a sunny recess close to the seashore. The living room, with a ceiling height of 3.7 metres, has an unhindered view of the sea and the small beach at the foot of the building, whereas the bedrooms are more sheltered. Sitting rooms and bedrooms are on the first floor, cantilevered from the base. This part of the building is clad with black-painted wooden boards with sliding panels that open to the sea towards the east, and the evening sun towards the west.

51

52

The interior and exterior reflect the scenic context of the house. The raw concrete constitutes a clear reference to the beach at the end of the plot, while the black-painted wooden facade significantly contrasts the grey concrete. The interior is characterised by the same theme, and utilises Douglas fir for flooring and furniture. **Casa Spodsbjerg** meets the applicable building regulation requirements in terms of energy.

Peacefully nestled in the lush green hills of Sai Kung (known as the 'Back Garden of Hong Kong'), this 4,550-square-foot house was completely remodelled to create a spacious, stylish and tranquil living space for its owners. **Millimeter Interior Design Limited** transformed an impractical and cramped split-levelled building into a four-storey home incorporating a garage, a large living room, a family room, two small en suite bedrooms, two guestrooms with one guest bath, a 'helper' room, a master en suite bedroom with a spacious walk-in closet and den, as well as an open rooftop sitting area with spectacular sea and garden views.

One of the major shortcomings of split-level homes is that the layout often divides the house into several distinct 'boxes' that make it difficult to connect spaces together. As a result, the non-traditional multistorey home becomes cramped and challenging to use effectively. **Millimeter Interior Design Limited**'s solution was to demolish the original structure and create a completely new space; the architect's intention was to not only enhance the visual and ambient augmentation of interior space, but to optimise and harmonise its use as both a comfortable home and a welcoming hub for social gatherings.

House in Sai Kung features a fully equipped open kitchen that was designed to extend downwards, creating a clutter-free space. The dining table is cleverly hidden at floor level and can be elevated when required to further enhance space usage, while a contemporary indoor glass garage adds an edge to the home's raw and stylish finish.

Being a host to frequent house parties, the owner wanted to provide ample space for his guests. The full ground floor stretches from the entrance out to the backyard deck and is separated by a large set of foldable glass patio doors overlooking a 5-metre-long swimming pool.

Denizen Works was commissioned to produce a design for a new house on the remote site of a ruined, B-listed black-house on the Isle of Tiree, on the west coast of Scotland (accessible from the mainland via ferry services or by air). They developed a concept that comprises two houses: a 'living-house' and a guesthouse, linked by a utility wing. Together the elements combine to create **House No. 7**, a bold insertion into the landscape that reflects the character and heritage of the island.

In keeping with the philosophy of **Denizen Works**, the language of the house was driven by an examination of the local vernacular, materials and building forms, with the architecture of the living-house and utility taking the lead from the local agricultural buildings that combine soft roof forms, chimneys and corrugated cladding. Setting off the utilitarian accommodation is the guesthouse: deep-set stone walls, a black and white palette and black tarred roof result in a building that is tied to the unmistakable landscape of Tiree.

The living-house, containing the living, kitchen and dining spaces, functions as the social heart of the new home. The living space is a half-level up from the entrance, while the master bedroom is sunk into the landscape, with views to the sheltered garden. Access to the garden – facilitated by the removal of the sand blow build-up around the existing cottage – and the beach is from the southern end of the space.

The guesthouse is constructed in the stone from the original cottage and contains two guest bedrooms, a bathroom and a quiet snug / entertaining room with an open link to the main hall in the utility. The utility is the functional heart of the building, containing laundry facilities along with a wet room (in which to clean off the sand from the beach) and a studio for painting and play. This third element, with the feel of a covered outdoor area, seamlessly links other spaces, allowing family and guests to interact as they choose.

The interior, which contrasts the robust architecture of the exterior, is filled with natural light. The finishes are intentionally sturdy, with inspiration for the palette taken from local Tiree architecture.

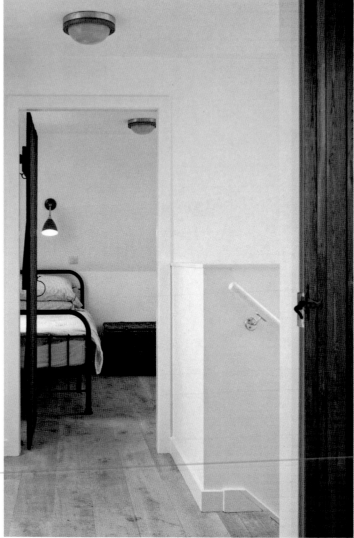

stanic harding architecture totally remodelled a dilapidated, unremarkable 1950s house on a waterfront property adjacent to Tarben Creek, Australia. The challenge was to create a light and airy home on this steep south-facing site while maintaining connections to the garden, water and city views.

A series of three distinct pavilions were formed – linked by two open courtyards – allowing **Hunters Hill House** to gradually step down the site. The courtyards allow sunlight to enter the house via the extensive glazing on the northern facades. The transparency and deep modulation of these facades offer protection from the summer sun, while permitting winter light to reach deeply into the house. The courtyards provide access to level gardens and external living spaces – crucial on such a sloping site.

The waterfront terrace of the original house was maintained to offer a connection to the waterfront garden and the city, water and bridge views beyond. Many existing trees and plants were retained by **stanic harding architecture**; the landscape design intent was to return the waters edge to its original state.

The use of the low-pitched skillion roof form exacerbated the house's subdued presentation to the harbour and neighbouring properties, while the street frontage was deliberately restrained, as a considered contemporary insertion, offering limited visual access to the house beyond.

This breathtaking site on the edge of a typical mountain hamlet in Valais, Switzerland, enjoys magnificent 360-degree views. Looking down the slope, rooftops of the village houses give way to an alpine panorama beyond; looking upwards, a succession of terraced pastures imbue the region with a tranquil atmosphere.

House Val d'Entremont is simple in shape: a rectangular cuboid with a roof which has two sloping sides, much like the traditional-style homes of the village below. It consists of three levels. The 'daytime' spaces on the intermediate level have open floor plans, with glazed floor-to-ceiling windows that capture natural light and offer spectacular vistas of the surroundings. Floors and ceilings comprise of brown stained concrete, with **Savioz Fabrizzi Architectes** lining one wall section with polished stainless steel to reflect the picturesque landscape.

The bedrooms on the level above and the small apartment on the level below are given a more abstract treatment via the use of white paints and resins. Exterior facades of weathered-finish wood will darken over time, taking on the same colour as the barns in the village, making **House Val d'Entremont** a timeless building that blends seamlessly into its locale, neither adding nor detracting from it.

Mirante do Horto House was strongly influenced by both national and international artistic movements, primarily Modernist and Bauhaus. **FCstudio** aimed to create spaces that enjoyed extreme flexibility and a wide visual range, meaning that the location of specific rooms and air circulation had to be carefully considered prior to construction.

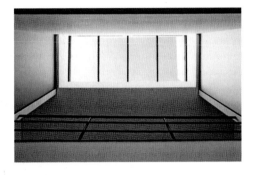

Located in São Paulo, Brazil, this 3,229-square-foot home rests on two yellow steel beams, allowing the architects to push the reinforced concrete house to the boundary of the small site. The garage – with a striking black slatted door – is tucked directly below these beams, further maximising the utilisation of site space. A gap between the earth and the base makes the house appear as if it is hovering, and allows light and air into the basement. Sculptural elements emerge from the roof to disrupt the orderliness of the building, while the smooth curve generated by the volume of the water tank and the copper triangle attic contrast in colour, texture and shape.

FCstudio kept the sleek, polished interior open; the interface between the kitchen, backyard and dining room blurs the borders in favour of a large common area. Skylights and light wells from the roof garden above bring abundant natural light to these high-traffic spaces, meaning the use of artificial light is not necessary during the day.

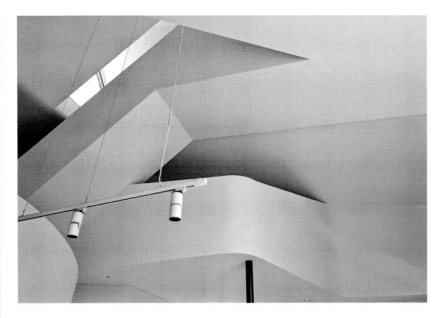

Walls sinuously move and bend through this loft apartment interior housed in a former butter factory, in West Melbourne, Australia. A sculptural stair sits at the converging point in the space, twisting and soaring up towards a recreational roof terrace, which overlooks the city of Melbourne.

Adrian Amore Architects' monochrome palate of white-on-white with charcoal and black plays with the abundant natural light drawn in from the large north-facing windows and ceiling void.

The essentially open ground-floor plan of **Loft Apartment** is defined by bending and wrapping walls that contain a bathroom, laundry and storage areas. Sliding doors create the opportunity for expanding and / or containing spaces, depending on how the ground floor is used, whether it be as a studio, bedroom or for entertaining.

Adrian Amore Architects have broken down conventional approaches to spatial planning in domestic architecture with **Loft Apartment**. Poetics of form are equally as important as function in this project, and both work symbiotically to create a streamlined, contemporary and innovative home.

Madrona House was designed as a summer retreat for a Bay Area couple who wanted to spend the warm summer months away from the San Franciscan fog. Built on a steep slope and a narrow lot, this 4,000-square-foot home is spread over three floors, with the master, guest and children's bedroom on the ground floor, and living spaces on the upper floor, taking full advantage of the spectacular views.

The main living level includes a large kitchen, dining and living space; it is connected to two home offices by way of a bridge that extends across the double-height entry, and brings filtered light – via skylights – down to the entry on the ground level.

All living space takes advantage of grand views of Lake Washington and the city skyline beyond. Two large sliding glass doors open up completely, allowing the living and dining space to extend to the deck outside. On the first floor, in addition to the guestroom, **CCS Architecture** included a 'kids room' – with two bunk beds and a separate bathroom – for visiting nieces and nephews. The basement level contains storage, a mechanical room and a two-car garage.

Nestled at the confluence of two creeks, **Mill Springs Ranch** is a water's edge retreat on an expansive ranch in Vanderpool, Texas. **Lake | Flato Architects** organised the four building elements around the site of the original ranch house and dam, resulting in a courtyard shaded by mature pecan trees and spaces with an intimate connection to the cool spring-fed creeks.

The main living area aligns to the geometry of the existing dam and provides dynamic views to the creeks and the valley landform they have shaped over time. The family bedroom wing serves as a mediating element between the creek and the natural valley landscape. Focusing on the main creek and pecan grove, the bedrooms leverage the two most treasured elements in the harsh Texas climate: water and shade.

Conceptually, the four elements are seen as artefacts linked to the existing dam. Masonry walls of locally quarried limestone anchor each space and form a sheltered courtyard while orienting the rooms to cooling breezes, views and landscape elements. Light steel and glass walls with large sliding doors provide **Mill Springs Ranch** with an immediate connection to the outdoors, or complete the enclosure of the spaces in response to the varying weather conditions.

Moebius House is 'future focused', open and responsive in approach, and experimental in nature. It faces views of Australia's Sydney Opera House and Harbour Bridge, and has a fluidity of space that is a direct result of its strong relationship with the surrounding landscape. Due to the complex geometry of the house, **Tony Owen Partners** had to evolve a completely new system of fabrication and assembly. In the end, the construction process more closely resembled that of a car. In traditional house construction, the floor and walls are built first, and the roof is added later. **Moebius House** was assembled around a chassis on-site and pre-formed metal cladding panels were attached to create a shell. The house is wired and plumbed like a car too, with the electrical, air conditioning and services all wired through the chassis. The kitchen even resembles a dashboard.

Moebius House was detailed and documented entirely in 3D. The steel frame was clad in metal panels, which were pre-cut in China, and the complex curving structure, like the ribs of the human body, had to fit within a very slim cladding zone; the margins were so tight that if anything was out by a few millimetres, the ribs would stick out from the skin.

With **Moebius House**, **Tony Owen Partners** explore an architecture, and indeed a lifestyle, which is more responsive to the environment. They call it 'Elastic Design': architecture that is pliant and capable of responding to all manner of changing variables – including spatial, programmatic, environmental and structural issues – but with an inherent structure and ordering principle. Thus the design of **Moebius House** creates spaces that expand to allow greater connectivity to the exterior environment – to maximise light, air and movement flows – and retract for greater privacy.

This attractive site on a slope borders generous meadows and offers views over the valley and the city of Altensteig in Germany. The striking facade of **Altensteig House** by **Kauffmann Theilig & Partner** – which is coated in Larch wood and rear-ventilated – includes metal inlays at vital points of the facade, added to accentuate important openings. Changes in light result in the appearance of different shadow effects, adding texture, colour and vibrancy to the wood-panelled exterior shell of this single-family residence.

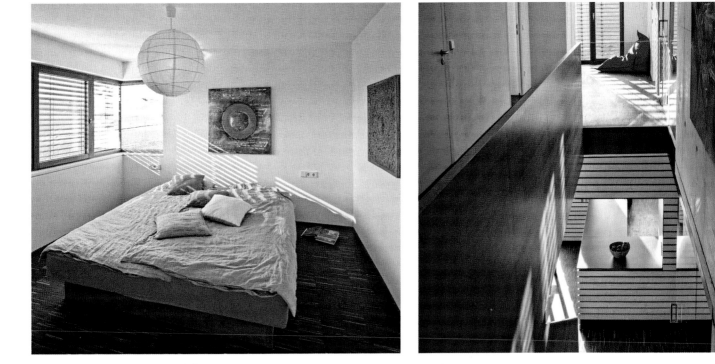

The ground floor – with entry, kitchen and living – is organised on three different levels, and is extended toward the outer terrace level at the south. The mainly orthogonal ground-floor scheme breaks open on the valley side with a moderate roof overhang and a transparent view to the surrounding forest.

Traditional materials of brick, concrete, limestone, steel and zinc were used by
Brininstool + Lynch to form this non-traditional house on a typical lot on the
north side of Chicago. *Claremont House* further resists city conventions by
uniting the front yard with the back using visual transparency; sheets of glass
more than 10 feet high and 14 feet wide terminate an open plan of 63 feet in
length on the first floor. A three-storey volume of millwork separates the floors from
the vertical circulation of the stairway and contains storage and equipment, neatly
separating functional performance from open space.

A stainless steel kitchen island used for cooking and dining is the only object built within the open space of the first floor. This area overlooks a courtyard, and the garage's vibrant green roof. The ground floor houses the guestroom and family room, and is framed by a large sheet of glass that brings the outdoor courtyard – visually – into the interior, flooding the area with ambient natural light. An outdoor stairway from the kitchen to the courtyard is wrapped with perforated zinc panels that shade southern light into the courtyard. Private rooms are located on the second floor.

118

Of the home's many green and sustainable features, the thermal mass of the concrete on the lower level provides natural cooling in warm weather, and is distributed by operable windows in alignment with the stairs. The open risers of the stair allow for continuous air movement, and with the strategic placement of windows, the stairway acts as a natural turbine, moving cool air from the lower level, and displacing warm air on the upper levels. In cool weather, the open risers allow warm air – generated from the radiant floor system of the lower level – to circulate upwards by the strategic placement of return-air ducts.

Elevated wooden boardwalks extending into the beachscape are a common occurrence in the dunes of Eastern Long Island, New York. Their simple construction challenges the extreme natural elements found at the intersection of land and sea, and they provide a unifying accessibility that connects the disparate elements of building and landscape. In the design for **Mothersill**, a vacation home in Water Mill, New York, **Bates Masi Architects** utilise the boardwalk as an architectural device for weaving together multiple portions of a historic site with new building and landscape elements.

Located on a creek-front property, the site contains two culturally significant structures – a small house and studio designed by architect Andrew Geller, built in 1962. A varied collection of botanically significant plantings also populate this property, including a rare specimen yew garden, serpentine yew hedge, and more than 400,000 Siberian irises. The western edge of the property slopes downward to a low-lying wetland bordering the creek.

The owners requested a design that seamlessly incorporated the protected Geller structures, Yew garden and new residence. Consequently, **Bates Masi Architects** incorporated a constructed path (recalling the boardwalks of Geller's architecture) that traverses the site to create visual and spatial relationships between these elements.

The path originates from the relocated Geller House in the Yew garden and winds around a serpentine hedge to a new swimming pool. As it continues, it passes the Geller Studio, now reprogrammed as a pool house, and connects to shaded outdoor living spaces. A new central lawn is defined as the boardwalk that wraps to extend through the main house, the end of which is enveloped by a cantilevered deck at the termination of the path, providing views of the sloping wetland and creek. The surface of the path then folds up and over to become the enclosure of **Mothersill**, with the same wood decking as the boardwalk simultaneously functioning as floor, wall and roof.

Located in the centre of Cascais, Portugal, this house's design on a narrow plot was informed by the dimensions of nearby summerhouses, which proliferated in the Portuguese coastline during the 40s, 50s and 60s. Lisbon-based **Humberto Conde Arquitectos** marked the new construction by aligning it with its surrounding buildings (with three floors above the ground and one basement), creating a strong dialogue with the locale. But the similarities end there. *Parede 11*'s aesthetic is stark and Modernist, and a definite departure from the rest of the streetscape, with white cement panels punctuated by elongated vertical windows, and hinged shutters integrated into the facade. At the front of the house, a gently sloping courtyard is large enough for two cars, while the back comprises a sophisticated patio with protective shrubbery and a lap pool, with a projecting balcony shading the interiors.

Inside, the colours of objects punctuate expanses of white, from walls and doors to built-in furniture, sinks and cupboards. Main living and dining areas are connected to the garden via full-height sliding doors.

This contemporary home north of Cape Town, in Yzerfontein, South Africa, is bordered by a nature reserve adjoining the ocean. Taking full advantage of the broad views and responding to the coastal context, **Gavin Maddock Design Studio** created a 600-square-metre, white, crisp, Minimalist home that perfectly reconciles house, dune and views.

The architecture and interiors were inspired by South Africa's West Coast landscape, which is typified by simple white houses and cottages reminiscent of the Mediterranean. Cavity brick construction was used throughout **Pearl Bay Residence**, with all walls plastered and painted white. Granite tiles were selected for their texture and grain, which resonates with rocks in the distance; they contrast with **Gavin Maddock Design Studio**'s softer, more subtle interiors, as do floor slabs of off-form concrete. Furniture was chosen for its scale and simplicity, as well as colour, shape and materiality; all are bold Modernist pieces that hold the spaces together well. In the living room, the television and audio equipment is cleverly concealed in a wall cabinet, behind a large steel-framed sliding panel that accommodates a substantial piece of artwork, and a custom-designed fireplace was recessed into a stainless steel ledge to accentuate a sense of spaciousness.

Striving to minimise the structure and maximise views, the interior-to-exterior opening that addresses the ocean was stretched to 14 metres, while ceiling heights of 3.3 metres further emphasise the feeling of lightness. Full-height sliding doors retract completely into the structure so that living areas flow seamlessly to the outside deck.

Pobble House takes its name from an old Kentish word for pebble and is located within the Dungeness Estate, a stark and open headland on the Kent and Sussex coast that is home to Europe's largest expanse of shingle – classifying it as Britain's only desert – and a vast array of wildlife and plant species. The area is recognised as a Site of Special Scientific Interest (SSSI), a National Nature Reserve, a Conservation Area and a Special Landscape Area. Owing to the site's cultural and natural significance, local planning policy dictates that any new building must replace an existing building and must be of similar scale and proportion to that of the original. For this reason **Pobble House** is made of three simple forms taken from the original dwelling.

Its main section is clad in Siberian larch and forms the central living, kitchen and dining areas, with bedrooms and bathrooms connected along a corridor running the home's length. A separate children's bedroom module located to the north is connected by glazing and is clad in cement fibreboard. The third section houses the building's main entrance to the home and dining area.

Guy Hollaway Architects chose materials carefully so that they reflect the surrounding vernacular of Dungeness. Larch cladding will weather silver over time with persistent high wind and salty sea air. The corten steel will rust to form a bright red protective coating, taking its cue from many exposed metal works that surround the site. In contrast to these natural materials, the separate bed module is clad in cement fibreboard and will not weather. **Pobble House** is also set on concrete pillars, which elevate the building from the site and serve to minimise any impact on the existing natural shingle surface.

Inside, the new home is organised along a linear corridor running the length of the building, and is aligned perfectly with the nearby lighthouse. From this, bedrooms and bathrooms maximise the building's small footprint and are orientated to maximise views from within. At its southern-most section a large open-plan kitchen, dining and living area form the heart of the home, with a bespoke log burner and a combination of large-format glazing and picture windows providing almost panoramic views over the spectacular site. In the living area, the corner of the building can be opened up to the landscape via a bespoke corner-to-corner glazed sliding door, which can be hidden within concealed wall pockets.

Santa Monica Canyon Residence is nestled into a hillside property in little Santa Monica Canyon, California. At the entry, a winding path provides enhanced perspective views and descends into an impromptu, landscaped amphitheatre. In the entry sequence of this path, the view through the house to the exterior space beyond is framed, offset, and then fully revealed at the doorway.

Griffin Enright Architects included a long skylight that extends the geometry of the path as it winds through the living space, illuminating open, loft-like living spaces with indirect natural light, and bending to visually link the front and back doors. As it moves through the house, sculpting the high ceiling, the skylight connects the two new courtyards created by the form of the residence.

At the rear facade, pocket doors disappear to frame the view of the exterior from the living room, while a deck at the rear has views into the living area and through the house to the front courtyard. The main living area's high ceiling compliments the view from the back courtyard, as the ceiling lifts and the longitudinal section parallels that of the descending geometry of the entry sequence. **Santa Monica Canyon Residence** is both held together as a whole and divided into parts by the volumetric carving of the skylight, and the exterior seems to pull through the house along the same path, as the visual continuity between the back and front courtyards is maintained along the zigzag spine of the structure.

Hog Pen Creek Residence is located northwest of downtown Austin, Texas, along Lake Austin. The project site was originally developed in the 1940s as a series of lakefront cabins. The challenging site slopes 26 feet down to the water and is distinguished by its large, sculptural oak and cypress trees. The building's footprint was defined by the Austin heritage tree ordinance, the river's restrictive flood plain and the adjoining creek and buildings.

As a triathlete, the owner envisioned a home that engaged with the outdoors, while accommodating spaces for off-season training. The design embraced the idea of access to much of the house coming from outdoor covered porches and walkways. Using the verticality of the old trees on-site, **Lake | Flato Architects** also created an inviting treetop experience.

149

The confined building footprint and slope of the land inspired the idea of a strong, axial boardwalk 'spine' that gently steps down with the slope of the land, providing access to many the areas of the house. This spine culminates in a two-storey outdoor living room, then terminates at the covered pavilion at the lake's edge.

The regulation-size lap pool – framed in a long horizontal window from the living room – is the centrepiece of the courtyard and a visual acknowledgment of the owner's passion for triathlon. The second-storey master bedroom sits at the level of the treetops and overlooks the screened porch and living room below. One office is located in a bay that projects over the swimming pool; the second is in a small glass box perched above the outdoor living room, with a crow's-nest view of the lake.

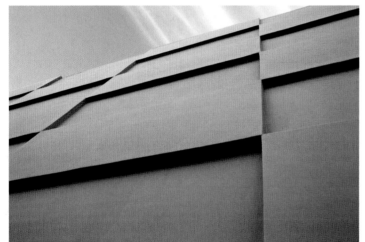

Goodman Residence epitomises the Southern California lifestyle by uniting the home, garden and pool. Its massing was conceived as one linear bar running the depth of the lot, which has two smaller masses attached to its side. The combination of the three masses, some open, some closed, sets up a dialogue of solid and void, covered and uncovered, indoor and outdoor, and creates an interaction and flow of functions.

The north facade enhances privacy with a sculptural composition of layered, smooth steel trowel stucco with minimal windows; while the courtyard facade is very open, organised in a horizontal pattern of phenoelic resin panels that shift in alignment with the window and door systems. Sliding and bi-fold doors on the courtyard open to allow access across the entire length of the compact 40'x135' urban lot.

The outdoor living spaces become rooms, some with roofs, some open to the sky, all partially enclosed either by the house itself, or the property-line walls. **Abramson Teiger Architects** sought to bring natural light into all parts of the home to imbue a sense of tranquility and lightness that make this home a private sanctuary.

Goodman Residence is situated on a long narrow lot; the design challenge was to position it accordingly in order to preserve an openness that is fully integrated both inside and out. The resultant massing is that of a long 'bar' with 'transparent' covered rooms added to it. A dialogue of solid and void, covered and uncovered, indoor and outdoor is established. The living room, with its tall doors that disappear into pockets, the garden courtyard and pool, and the outdoor covered patio are aligned to allow clear visuals from one end of the site through to the other. Natural light plays an important part in the space, helping to imbue the home with an airiness and quietness, thus transforming ***Goodman Residence*** into a private sanctuary. Attention was also paid to articulating the 'bar' by creating a visually interesting, sculptured exterior.

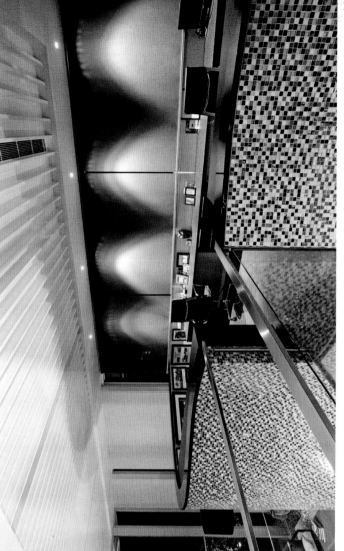

This sleek beachside house orientates towards the northern boundary to take advantage of the sun and prevailing sea breezes, while a two-storey void – with views to the sky – was incorporated to allow light and air to penetrate the long floor plan. The bedrooms on the first floor look into the living area and pool below, facilitating a sense of openness, and the study, located above a magnificent curved mosaic element, houses the laundry and guest bedroom below.

The owners requested a design that reflected the qualities of a permanent urban residence, rather than a holiday house. Internally, **Paul Uhlmann Architects** integrated finishes like polished concrete, tiled walls and stained timber to reflect the functional and contemporary direction of the aesthetic. The position of the curved mosaic entry wall was spatially and aesthetically balanced with the fluidity of the overall design. *Surf Residence*'s external cladding of furniture-grade Hoop pine chamfer board and shiplap spotted gum cleverly compliments the character of the region's beach houses and gives the building a local identity.

American Modernist architect Barry Dierks built numerous villas on the French Riviera between 1925 and the 1950s. His architecture remains a characteristic feature of the Mediterranean coastline to this day, particularly as most of his buildings are heritage protected. One of the best-known owners of one of his villas was British novelist and playwright William Somerset Maugham. Barry Dierks designed the first building in this series, the *Villa Le Trident*, in 1926 for himself and his partner and lived there with him until his death.

Villa Le Trident was sold in 2011. German architects **4a Architekten** received the commission to completely renovate the building. They focused on preserving Barry Dierks' architectural legacy while giving the ageing villa a more contemporary ambience. The 'white, cubic architecture' of the villa's exterior continues to captivate. **4a Architekten** picked up on this distinctive aesthetic and developed it further, but in a contemporary manner.

Since the redesign, the prevailing impression is one of spaciousness, the suffusion of light and simple elegance. A large section of the interior walls on the ground and first floors were removed to create a fluid transition between the two spaces. The living and dining area – with an open-plan kitchen as well as a library – are located on the ground floor. The first floor includes four bedrooms with en suites. Long window facades offer superb views of the sea. White suspended furniture, white curtains on external walls, solid oak floorboards and glass elements lend a bright and tranquil atmosphere to the rooms. Distinctive features include a fireplace suspended from the ceiling, and a wall-design element designed by **4a Architekten** in the library. Teak-panelled freestanding cubes are another eye-catching feature on both floors.

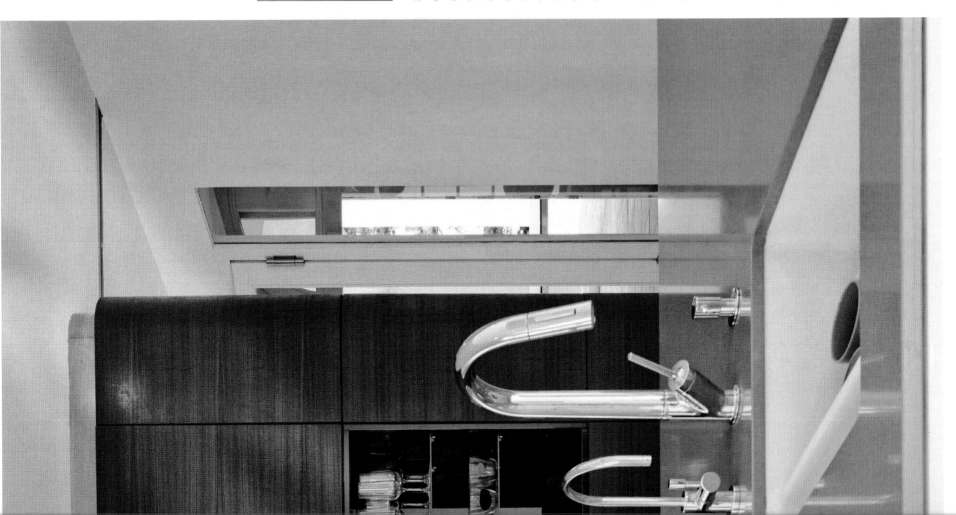

In order to retain **Villa Le Trident**'s splendid views, the bathroom and dressing rooms vertical ducts were detached from external walls and integrated into the teak cubes. The linear lighting along their bottom edges brings out the character of the fitted furniture, creating atmospheric illuminated highlights within the room. Sliding glass doors were installed, allowing the sea views from the long window facades to remain uninterrupted, and to emphasise fluidity and space.

The house is one of a row of detached Federation houses built in 1901 and sits on ridge overlooking Cooper Park in Sydney, Australia. The frontages are mostly intact, however the rears of the properties facing north are diverse in both character and quality. *Wollahra House 1* was badly renovated in the 1970s and, as such, only the front street-facing room and street facade were retained. **stanic harding architecture** completely removed all other structures and excavated a new floor level under the existing street entry level for the inclusion of a pool. The street frontage also had to be fully restored; the architects endeavoured to create a contrasting contemporary rear facade that would address both the northern aspect and the nearby park. The edge treatment of the new rear balcony quite literally frames these views.

The small scale of **Wollahra House 1**'s footprint meant the need for careful spatial connections, both horizontally and vertically, to extend the available space. A new slatted light court replaces the existing front terrace, while floor level changes, joinery elements and ceiling treatments create and conceal spaces.

Ulm House, which sits on a former fruit orchard in the northwest of Ulm, Germany, is characterised by its topography – a slope to the south, a forest to the north and undeveloped green space to the west. It is from this existing arrangement that the functional partitioning and the formal appearance of this family house evolved – closeness to nature, privacy and family spaces were key criteria.

A transparent basement opens to the garden; above this, **Kauffmann Theilig & Partner** have placed two irregular volumes – closed to the exterior – that aesthetically mirror clasps. Cars travel via a subsurface tube to the basement. The ground floor has all the common functions of a typical family home. It was designed as an open transparent space with fluid transitions to the garden, pool and terrace. Different room heights – a direct result of ceiling offsets and level changes – shape the atmosphere of the interior space as a whole. The separate areas in the house devoted to relaxing, eating, children and parents are layered from the bottom up, and each area is arranged around a shared central space. Half-storey galleries over the living space are staggered with open balustrades that lead to the common space. Parquet flooring emphasises the flowing transition by continuing to outdoor areas.

Working within the bones of a solid, well-constructed waterfront home built in Australia in the 1960s on Sydney's Parramatta River, the adaptive reuse of this multilevel dwelling involved removing the internal workings of the existing structure, re-invigorating the central circulation core and promoting light and cross ventilation while embracing the waterfront outlook to the northwest.

Tennyson Point Residence is arranged over four levels, cascading from the road frontage towards the water's edge through a series of lofty indoor and outdoor living spaces, which reveal unique harbour views. **CplusC Architectural Workshop** divided the home into two distinct areas: private and social. Private bedroom spaces are located in the timber-clad volume to the front of the site, affording privacy to the street while opening toward spectacular views across Morrison's Bay. The living and entertaining areas are located further down the site, and are linked by two large masonry walls retained from the original structure. These spaces provide a series of open sun-lit terraces, and have a physical connection to the landscaped waterfront recreation area, as well as the swimming pool and deck. Large operable doors and windows visually connect the internal spaces to the immediate site, allowing these areas to open out to the bay and imbue the rooms with a sense of openness and connection to place.

The materials chosen were informed by the desire for a warm, natural aesthetic and a healthy living environment free from artificial and chemical finishes. Externally, the extensive use of timber grounds the building while sandstone salvaged from the demolition was utilised in the new works. The recycled masonry elements include a new sea wall to Morrison's Bay in addition to other landscape elements.

The series of terraces and platforms throughout the site include over 4.5 kilometres of hardwood decking. Internally, the use of timber has been moderated with the inclusion of a crisp, clean, modern palette of materials, including sparkling white Corian and stainless steel bench tops, natural limestone tiles and painted surfaces.

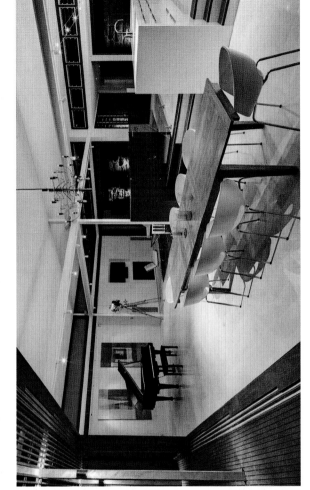

Morscher Architekten converted former Art Deco chapel, **St. Luke's**, built in 1924 in Bern, Switzerland, (and totally disfigured in a 1970s renovation) into two new homes. In order to keep the ground floor free of supports, and retain the natural light from the high church windows, the upper apartment was 'hung' as a concrete cube in the former double-storey nave, resulting in a striking, contemporary aesthetic.

The previously closed south facade was opened up with generous sliding windows and projecting balconies looking onto the neighbourhood and the garden. Both spaces were also equipped with simple Minergie® ventilation systems that facilitate the interface between living and sleeping areas, bringing in fresh air and drawing off stale air through wall vents.

Originally from Gujarat, India, the clients wanted a large dwelling that would accommodate extended family visits, while incorporating elements of the rich traditions of their homeland. Drawing on Indian architectural precedents, such as stone domes, step-wells and temple towers, **Lakeshore Residence** blends subtle Indian influences with a clean, modern sensibility.

The white stone that extends throughout the house is reminiscent of many of the great historical buildings of India. **Miró Rivera Architects** responded with a composition that combines white stone with copper outside and wood inside. The starkness of the white stone is softened by the inclusion of warmer, more tactile accents of Makore and Pearwood throughout the house. The glass stairs and second-floor walkway tie the public and private spaces together in a contemporary material that allows light to penetrate the double-height space of the gallery.

An equally essential part of the project was the inclusion of water features. The architects started by incorporating views of the lake in nearly all of the interior and exterior spaces, and continued by bringing water into the property in the form of a 5,000-square-foot pond off the master bedroom and terrace. Water is also integrated into the entry sequence via a large reflecting pool that surrounds the foyer, office and 'prayer room', and cascades into a smaller reflecting pond and fountain that greets visitors.

Miró Rivera Architects were involved in aesthetic choices at all levels – from the design of the home and spaces to the selection of the china patterns. The dining room features a custom dining table designed by the architects, while the central outdoor room includes a pair of custom-built swings that allow residents to enjoy the expansive views of the lake. The bedroom's built-in bed, nightstands and headboard were also custom-designed by the architects and are made of Pearwood.

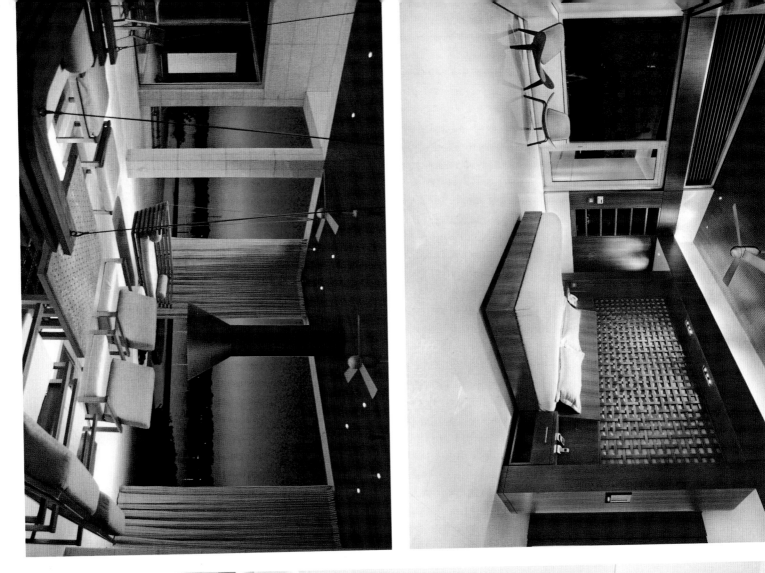

Planalto House in São Paulo, Brazil, could be considered as exemplary of current Brazilian contemporary architecture. The building is defined by two large perpendicular volumes and is further divided into rectangular prisms, with overhanging slabs featuring prominently in the design. The upper floor is stacked as if balancing on the lower level, which acts as a structural support. To emphasise the house's 'weightless' appearance, **FCstudio** employed heavy, industrial materials, including 20-centimetre-thick concrete slabs, large metal beams and structural pillars.

The front entrance leads directly in to a 1.8-metre-wide corridor located under a large overhang off the main floor, through to an indoor pavilion and a barbeque / recreation area. **FCstudio** placed the top floor orthogonal to these spaces and this single point of contact creates a strong vertical connection between the home's different levels.

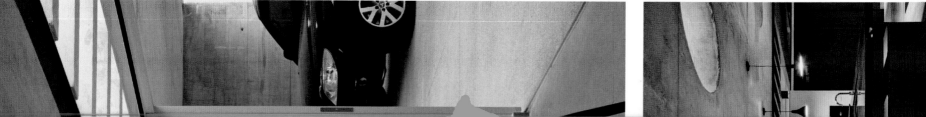

Bays of double-height windows at the stairs frame the room below, and reinforce **FCstudio**'s concept of two completely independent volumes. The use of elemental materials like wood, glass, concrete and steel create textures and transparencies that both complement and contrast one another – the sturdier materials delineating spaces, and the softer ones bringing the exterior into the house and vice versa.

Millimeter Interior Design Limited transformed the structure of an existing 40-year-old house to create a sophisticated, urban, modern home in Sha Tin, China. The highlight of **House in Shatin**'s thoroughly modern design is that it incorporates a sustainable green approach to reduce its environmental impact. The external walls of the house were rebuilt over the original, preserving the core structure and saving on building and reconstruction costs, while also reducing waste. The architects also planted a small Maple tree in the centre of house, facilitating an interaction between natural elements and living spaces. An open roof above the tree nourishes with sunlight and disperses natural light into the glass partitioned study room.

All lights in the house are automatically turned off when no one is present, and aluminium panels were installed to prevent sun heat from entering the house, reducing the use of air conditioners. In addition to this, large solar panels were installed on the rooftop to provide power to water heaters, lighting and backup batteries.

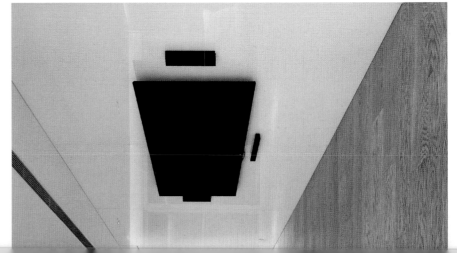

R.J. Melman Residence is a classic compact townhouse on a quiet street in Chicago's downtown area. Due to the fact that the owner is a well-known restaurateur in Chicago, loves cooking and is interested in interior design, **MOD Construction** and **Dirk Denison Architects** tried to accommodate his interests and make the house as comfortable as possible.

The first floor has space limitations, with an entryway designed so that it naturally guides guests away from the exercise room and towards the stairway to the second floor. The gym side has carpeted flooring and mirrored walls. It is separated from the stairway by a custom-designed, stained-oak shelving system.

An open concept living / dining room and kitchen on the second floor, with dark hardwood floors stained to match the millwork colour, provide a solid platform for the open space design. The living room has a charcoal-black fireplace finished with honed Black Absolute granite tile. Complementing the design are built-in floor-to-ceiling bookshelves for the owner to place all his design and culinary books and magazines.

The second-floor kitchen has a very conservative but contemporary style and colour palette, and includes a large island with wood veneer cabinets and appliances underneath a 3-inch-thick dark walnut butcher-block countertop. Four mint / red lights merge a traditional pendant shade and a wire-cage into an industrially inspired but refined feature. The style accent of the entire space is stainless steel kitchen cabinets and shelves along the east wall designed specially according to the owner's specifications.

MOD Construction's solution to the mediocre view from the south window (a brick wall) was a 'window box' lit by three semi-flush ceiling lamps, perfect for displaying the owner's artwork. The dining room has smoked eucalyptus cabinets along the east wall to match the cabinetry in the kitchen along the west wall, and a hidden door to the powder room.

The powder room has a unique retro atmosphere with mocha-coloured linen vinyl wall covering and smoked eucalyptus panels (matching the kitchen cabinetry) on the east wall. The floor and remaining walls are clad in charcoal-coloured Clifton Slate tile, while two ceiling-mounted Neutron light fixtures (clear acrylic cylinders with a satin nickel finish) brighten the mirror with a punch of white light. The master bathroom looks spacious due to the use of light colours, large square floor tiles and rectangular wall tiles. A long custom-made vanity cabinet, made of rift white oak with pre-finish maple interiors, has a white Carrara marble countertop that matches the walls.

Located in a residential area in Kuwait City, **Mop House**'s rectangular site can be accessed from either side of the surrounding streets, allowing for a residence with both private and public entrances. The form of the house is reminiscent of the movement patterns of a mop, from which flexible volumes are organised diagonally around a central axis. This axis twists upwards to generate spaces that channel views into different directions, including the front of the house, the side gardens and angles of the back street. Originally planned as a residence for one family with two small children, **AGi architects** designed **Mop House** to respond to both current and future needs – the client plans on dividing the residence into two individual units at a later date.

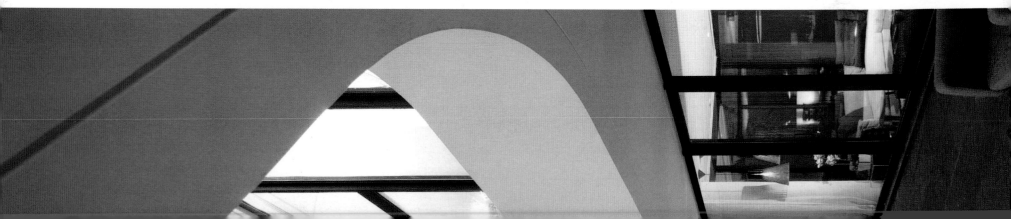

The ground-floor facade is clad in dark brown natural sandstone, while the upper levels are finished using white plaster to visually differentiate the lower portion and upper volume of the house. Bamboo is the main material present in the interior spaces, covering many of the curved walls and creating continuity and uniformity between separate areas. It also dominates the flooring on the first and second floors, providing private spaces with texture and warmth. On the ground level, both the interior and exterior feature the same dark stone flooring, which contrasts the swimming pool's lighter coloured tiles, and creates a sharp and refreshing aesthetic. The interiors of **Mop House** were designed by **AGi architects** in collaboration with Gunni & Trentino, a Spanish furniture manufacturer and supplier.

stanic harding architecture altered this modest, free-standing Californian bungalow in McMahons Point, Sydney, Australia, so it could accommodate a growing family. The house was, initially, unremarkable; it had no strategy in place that facilitated a connection to the limited outdoor space available, the entry was poorly defined and a carport attached to its base compromised its connection to the street. The architects worked in close collaboration with a heritage consultant, and used the accepted method of insertion and addition via contrast to its full effect.

An asymmetrical addition was designed to balance and compliment the existing silhouette. Initial discussions determined that the new object should be set back from the front of the existing house, thereby reinforcing the conservation zone streetscape objective. Its somewhat free form determined a material choice of zinc, an advantage due to the 'recessive' quality of its colour.

The front of **McMahons Point House** was expanded and the streetscape connection improved by a new half-level deck and street wall treatment. An entry sequence was inserted that provided few clues as to the zinc element overhead – this was done to reduce the scale of the house when moving down the side passage to the garden. The interior spaces were adjusted to improve function and allow for a more considered connection to new outdoor living areas. Existing elements of worth, like the bay window, were incorporated into the revised design scheme.

For **Brininstool + Lynch**, designing this Chicago residence was an exercise in creating privacy within an urban neighbourhood, while providing an abundance of open, bright space. The first floor is defined by clear views from the landscape to the back courtyard. Abundant northern and eastern light filters into private spaces on the second floor, while the third floor provides solitude for working; adjacent outdoor areas encompass views over the courtyard, the neighbourhood, and to the city skyline. Together, they comprise a rational and inspiring response to the basic human needs of living, sleeping and working.

Wood House is organised in an L shape. On the first floor, the two-storey living room includes a lay-light of patterned acrylic that filters natural daylight from the skylight above. Full-height windows and doors line the east and west sides of the room, creating a seamless link between indoors and out. Weathered copper panels hang above the fireplace in the living room and continue to the exterior, where two operable panels facilitate outdoor storage and stair access to the roof deck.

The other leg of the L is a three-storey volume along the north side of the property. Millwork boxes separate first-floor functions. Acoustical plaster was used on higher ceilings, while the lower millwork ceilings have a random, perforated square pattern that absorbs sound – a derivative of the pattern seen on the exterior copper screen. Black granite defines the perimeter circulation, and blocks of end-grain walnut infill the centre floor areas. Natural light is brought to an elegant open riser stair via a skylight.

229

The third floor is accessed via a simple wooden staircase behind a flush millwork door at the end of the second-floor hallway, and houses a private study and guest suite. Each space has its own deck and green roof with views to the sky and courtyard below. Here the windows are a continuous band of butt-glazed clerestories that provide an ethereal quality of light to the interior. The views, copper screens, connections to the exterior and careful detailing create a serene and distinctive environment.

In Greek, a Hemeroscopium is a place where the sun sets – a space defined by the sky and horizon. Living up to its name, **Hemeroscopium House** plays a game with gravity and balance, placing seven heavy structures in an apparently unstable formation that encloses living spaces. **Ensamble Studio** has created a magnificent (and surreal) house that truly pushes the boundaries; **Hemeroscopium House** is a new language in modern residential architecture in Spain.

The order in which these structures have been 'piled' generates a helix that branches from a stable support (the 'mother beam') and develops upwards in a sequence of elements that become lighter as the structure grows, closing on a point that culminates in equilibrium. The apparent simplicity of the structure's joints are deceiving; they required the development of complex calculations regarding the reinforcement, and the pre-stress and post-tension of the steel rods that connect the web of beams. **Hemeroscopium House** reaches equilibrium with what **Ensamble Studio** calls 'the G point', a 20-tonne granite stone that acts as a counterweight to the whole structure.

(**Hemeroscopium House** took one year to engineer but only seven days to build, thanks to the total prefabrication of the different elements and their perfectly coordinated assembly.)